DEARLY DIVORCED

DEARLY DIVORCED

poems

AMY BOLDING

*Dedicated to anyone
who has ever experienced heartbreak and loss.*

CONTENTS

INTRODUCTION

Whoever said divorce is the easy way out is either a liar or does not know the truth of it. The idea is heartbreaking before the decision is made. Divorce is a choice to burn down the bridges of your life, watching everything fall apart, and trying desperately to make the best of it as you pick up all the pieces along the way.

The process is gruesome and excruciating; like one can imagine losing a limb might be. One must learn to be alone. Strong bonds are torn apart, after years of taking form. A lot must be forgotten, or it's impossible to heal. It takes time to learn to live without the other half of you.

Just like the old song says, "Can't go over it, must go through it," you cannot escape the cascade of emotions that will flood your days. You must go through each variation of emotion and process it too. No, walking away isn't easy at all. Trauma is suffered by the brain and the heart.

I imagine that most artists consider their work as a labor of love, whereas I would consider this work a labor of pain. Much like bringing a child into the world, it can be excruciating, yet necessary. I hope you will move through the pages finding some peace and healing, while also knowing how necessary these poems were for my own healing. I am honored you are going on the journey with me.

With love,
Amy Bolding

PROLOGUE

DEATH

DEARLY DIVORCED,

We are gathered here today not only to mourn the loss of love, but the loss of our futures that were attached to it. The future we so fervently planned. The future we wholeheartedly put our faith into. The one that has now been shattered.

Maybe our futures were stolen from us by another. Maybe we walked away. Or maybe the rug was pulled out from underneath us. No matter, all of it has come to an end. When love dies, it is a slow death—much like the stages that follow the loss of love.

Move through the stages of grief with me now. Let them move you. We will walk in this together and recount all the ways that love slipped through our fingers.

Today, we grieve.

Unraveled

I unravel myself,
but what I reveal, you don't see.
Every emotion belonging to you
as good as remains a secret to me.

I dance and sing my songs of love,
in a rhythm that is not seen.
I hope and I plead
but your deaf ears reveal how much I am failing.

A Loveless Affair

Days go by without more than a glance.
No words of love shared or which to reply.
No touch of affection as I reach to turn out the nightstand
light. Only a peck on the cheek with a brief *Goodnight.*

And we expect one another to guess and know,
that love still lives there,
as if love runs on its own.

In the beginning, everything was right.
Conversations came easy.
Dinners were for lovers.
Love was made, both day and night.

But now, here we sit with babies and bills,
work every morning,
countless messes and spills.

The little ones play on the floor.
Our nerves are shot.
Our wallets are tight.
bodies are sore.

Somehow, we forgot
how to hold one another.
Surviving life is a priority, while loving is not.

There once was a time for passionate lovers.
But now they are like ghosts—
barely knowing one another,
existing without being seen.

Lovers Quarrel

Skin so close that I could touch you,
but I can't.
I won't.

Tensions lay heavy,
like a weighted blanket.
It's suffocating.

Like wearing a winter coat
on a summer's day;
unnecessary.

I loathe you,
but I want you near me.
Ego says, *pull away.*

My heart breaks
when you don't reach for me.
Throughout the night, I make silent apologies.

You'll never hear them—
the things I really mean—
as you spitefully sleep with your back to me

Each slight is a point:
either a trophy for my ego,
or salt in my wounds.

Questions

Why do I keep holding out for something to change?

Who are you?
Who am I?
Where should my heart draw the line?

Why do I stand at the crossroads, waiting for you to decide?
What am I waiting for?
Your return? Your arrival?
When is it appropriate to say, enough is enough?

Who is at fault if this breaks?
Why do I continue to beg you to stay?
Why am I so afraid to walk away?

Numbered Days

Come right out and tell me our days are numbered.
I press against you, but still feel lonely.

Years have passed without your fingers drawing circles on my skin.
Without sweet words falling on my ears,

I swear on my grave that I love you.
You swear on yours that you love me too.

But love knows it was lust all along—
You and I know it too.

The wind has no remorse for blowing so strongly.
The winter does not mind hanging around a little longer.

My lover doesn't reach for my hand.
And to him, it's no bother.

Hard to Tell

The good days bleed into the bad, and I start to wonder
if I'm crazy. I wonder through blurred, tear-filled eyes
if I am seeing things straight.

Because there's no way to differentiate
between the secrets you keep, and the lies I tell myself.

Praying

Every day, I prayed.
For you, for us,
for you to turn and notice
that I'm standing right beside you.
For you to see my value,
and to want me too.

Every morning, I prayed we stayed whole.
I begged for you to see me, to see us,
heading in a direction that was dangerous. My
chasing turned you away even more than before.
And now we all feel abandoned and cold, walking
away and thrust into the unknown.

From Dreaming to Dead

With a dream and a prayer,
A life was built.
The lovers had made it,
but that was until,

a heart began to wander,
with the other unknowing
a betrayal was coming,
discontent was growing.

She is stuck behind,
maintaining the world they'd spun.
While she was on cloud nine,
his deceit had only just begun.

One heart clings to perfection,
while the other's attention
not only is fading
but swings in a different direction.

Together, they will tear down everything that is good,
and thus, the tragedy
of wandering heart's eyes.
In the end, everyone loses, and everything dies.

I.

ANGER

Paper Houses

When did I begin to see my world falling apart?
From the beginning, if I am honest.
But there was no time, you see,
to really question any validity
because we had just begun to build it,
and I wanted to give things a chance.

So we built our house of love on lies and sand.
The outside walls looked as if they were painted in gold,
but inside they were all crumbling.
So I continued plastering the walls falling all around me,
all while singing the praises of this life,
and thinking I was lucky.

Little fires started here and there.
Not knowing what was normal,
I put them out and tried to forget.
There were moments when everything looked alright,
but buried deep beneath was the truth we both denied.

One day, to myself I would say, *One day I might have to walk away.*

Instead, I tried to fix it.
Scrambling here and there behind you,
wondering in each moment if I was too much or not enough.
I never really did know.
You hardly noticed.
You were too busy holding the torch that burnt it all down.

Hypocrite

Brush my lips with the same hands that held me down—
kept me silent, and under your thumb.

Fondle my hair with the same fingers that picked up my heart—
just to drop it. Over and over again.

Tell me you love me with the same breath that puts me down.
The same breath that swears your love to others.

Dream beside me as you single-handedly tear down
all the dreams we built together.
While I lose sleep over the revelations coming to light.

Do Not Resuscitate

Do not resuscitate.

This is more than a lover's quarrel.

Love shouldn't be this hard. This

is a battle.

This is a fight to the death,

and I've been fighting—

for me, for you, for everybody.

Now, it's me against you.

True love died long ago.

These are our final moments.

I've pulled the plug.

I've had enough.

Smoke & Beauty

*I read our vows before I burned them.
Wouldn't you know it, smoke follows beauty.*

*Fire swallowed the paper up in moments-
beautiful words which lost their importance.*

*Gone in an instant.
Who knew they were that easy to destroy?*

*Oh yeah. . .
you did.*

Hand and Heart Bleeding

And they all go away,
use you up, then spit you out.
Then we're left, with hands that are bleeding,
empty,
exhausted from holding it all together.

What was it all for?
Did you get what you wanted?
You came on strong, just to let us down.

You knew what you were doing,
using me up,
while keeping a short leash.

Was it worth it?
Preying on the little girl within me?
Did stealing the life out of me do anything?

How dare you get defensive
against a truth that was always going to come out. Taking

a closer look at you was the only thing that saved me.

Burn It

The vows that I helped you write.

The pictures of us that were hung on the wall.

The flowers from our wedding day.

The sign with our last name.

Burn it all.

Just A Pile

This home, no longer ours,
used to feel safe and warm.
Now it's empty and cold.

It's just a pile of walls and boards, concrete and stone.
But for this pile, we prayed—
envisioned, worked towards, and eventually obtained.

Just for you to throw it all away.
You shit on it, and on us too.
Then left behind the mess you made.

Ghost

I see a man, who is like a ghost.
One who stands before me, but who I cannot touch.
I catch glimpses of his last minute motions, but I
can see right through them.
Meaningless, for they were all too late.
And I sigh and shake my head at what could've been—
no longer a man, only dead to me.

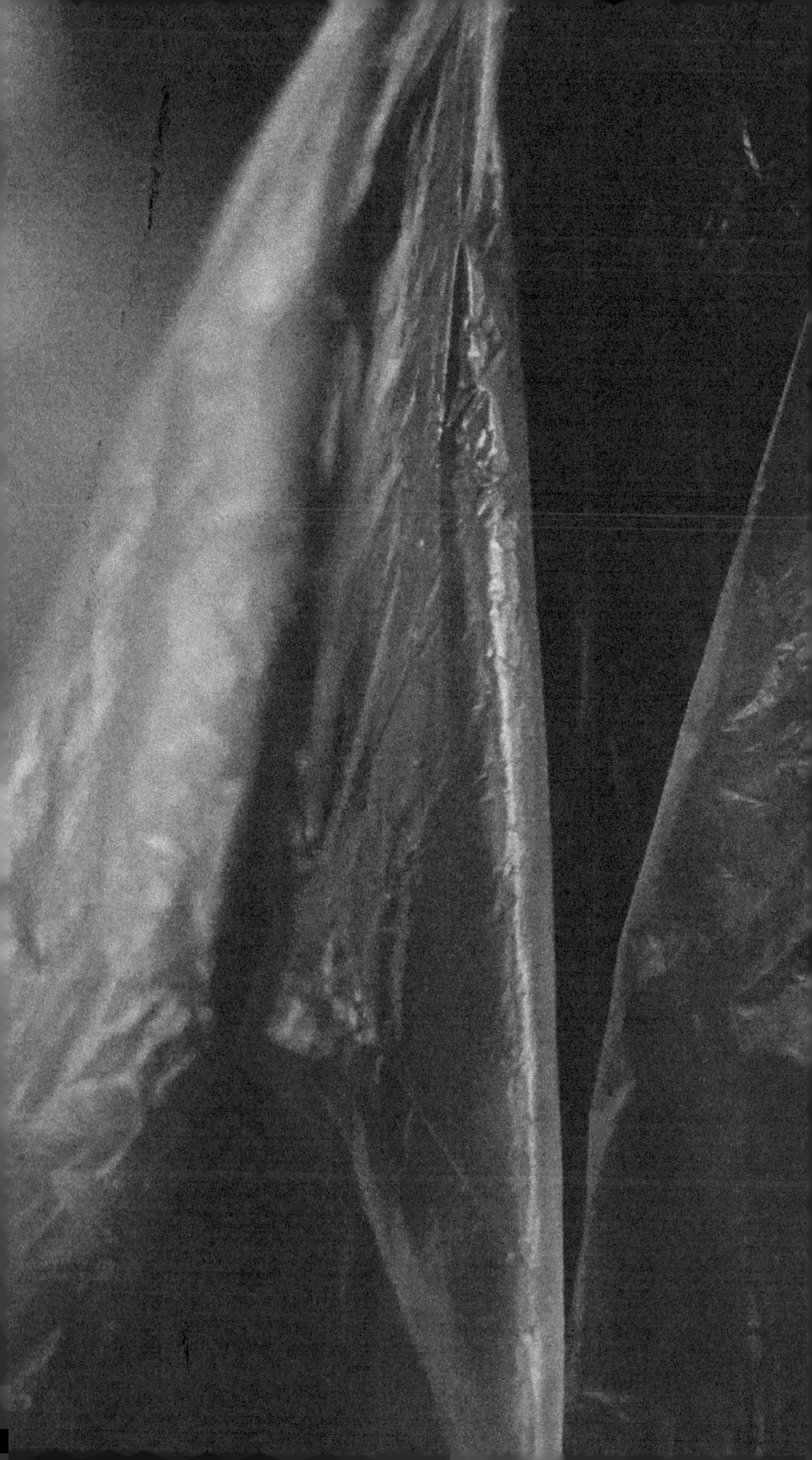

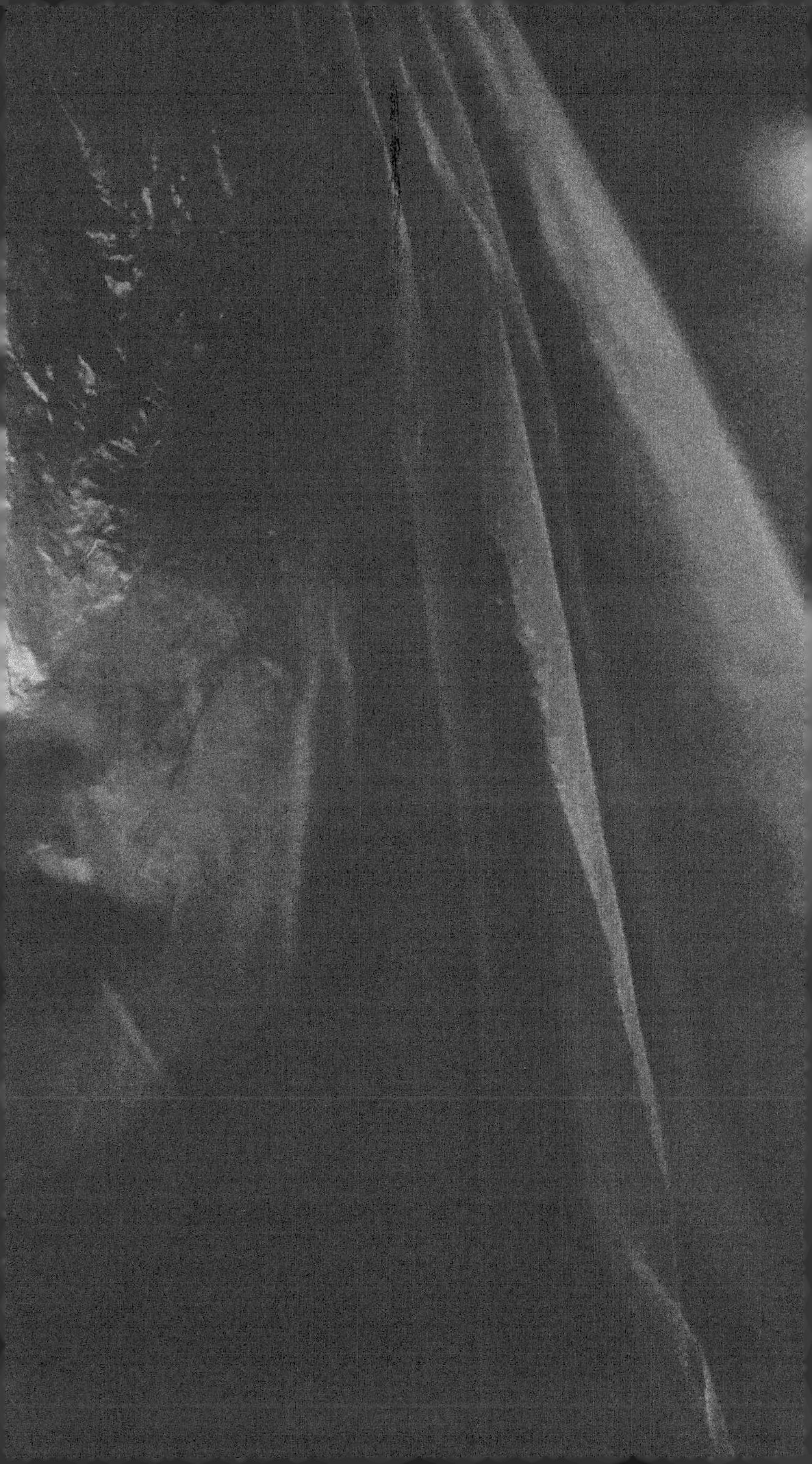

Excerpt of a Wife's Diary

Nights full of worry.
Lies the next day.
Forgetting for the sake of the family.

Complaints.
Complexities.
Everything withered away.

I let parts of me break,
even when I knew better.
Even when I knew you'd let us down.

Praying.
Pleading.
Crying over someone who didn't care.

This love has lost its luster,
and I've gained new sight.
My heart has been broken for the last time.

If The Phone Doesn't Ring, You Know It Was Me

If the phone doesn't ring, you know it's me.
No name on your screen.
No need for waiting.

If the call never comes, you know where my heart belongs.
Miles away from turning around.
Miles away from saying I was wrong.

If you're lonesome tonight, I can't make it right.
Too many bad memories.
Too far out of sight.

If your heart is breaking, I am not the glue.
No way for me to touch it.
No way I ever could.

Particles

You used to be my whole world.
My sun and my stars too.
But I took my heel and smashed that world to pieces.
Now we're just particles,
floating in space,
trying to find a place to land.

II.

BARGAINING

New Life Prayer

Breathe new life into us, Lord,
the way you bring new leaves in the spring.
May our deep roots hold on through all the freezes.
Heal us from the wounds we left on one another.
Lighten our burdens and scars,
so we can find one another again.

Truce

By now the pain has summoned
the darkest parts of me.
I will do anything to get away
from the constant stinging.

I need to find the answer
on how to make it stop.
If only I could go back in time
to save my broken heart.

If only there was a solution
on how to fix our life.
I don't know where to start
or how to make things right.

Neither God
nor the Devil
have shown up,
holding a better deal.

Let's just call a truce
and pretend it all away,
with hearts half-glued,
salvaging all that we may.

A Negotiation

The price to hold each other's hearts was too high.
Let's re-negotiate the vows we shared that night.

You'd agree to being more.
I'd agree to complaining less.

Let's try our luck—
each of us bending until we are unstuck.

We misunderstood what each one expected.
Trust was broken, but you confessed.

So I wonder if we could move past it—
new promises might make us forget…

By swallowing truths,
a gray area lets me hang onto you.

Go Tell Them

Little bird, can you go tell them
that I am weeping?
And that my tears
carry into the night,
when I tuck our children in
after telling them goodnight.

Dear darkness, please send a message
that says I am cold without them, and
that my anger has begun to fade.
Maybe I was just too dramatic.
Thoughts of them keep me awake.

Dear heart, please keep a secret.
It's between you and me.
I feel torn in different directions,
and I might be regretting
everything.

The Truth

If I'm being honest with myself,
I'd admit that I miss you.

You hurt me deeply,
and if I'm being honest,
it was in all the ways I knew you would.

Truth be told,
if you'd ask me today,
I cannot guarantee I'd walk away.

The fly on the wall knows I love you,
these walls have seen me cry over you,
although I pretend it's not true.

I don't understand a thing—
how we got here,
or what we are going through.

Maybe it's falling apart
to all come together,

We might have been wrong all along.

Crossroads

A decision must be made. Will
it kill me, or bring me life?

The answer,
unknown,
is breaking me apart.

The Reckoning,
grim,
is scaring me to death.

Unbroken Circles

I tried on my rings today,
to remember how they fit.
And my heart began to break.

What a pretty set.

The circles remained unbroken,
undisturbed by the mess we made.

What words should've remained unspoken
and replaced with love instead?

I tried imagining
how the future would play out
if decisions could be un-made,
and you knew the right things to say.

I try to see past all the hurt,
until I realize, it's all that's left.

Broken Homes

Wouldn't it have been nice if the fairytale were real?
And if there wasn't a trail of heartbreak, and we had
made a happy home,
instead of a mess?

So that every other weekend,
the halls in my home were not empty,
and when I walk past quiet, clean rooms
I wouldn't have to weep.

Wouldn't it have been nice if we had gotten along?
If my emotions didn't cause you to be overwhelmed
And I knew that yours actually existed?

It would've been nice to sit together at dinner,
talking about our days,
instead of arguing through the phone,
and tucking our children in separately.

III.

DENIAL

Lost Love

Losing love is not an explosive act—
doesn't come with a bang.
The separation of souls is black.
Darkness expands with every change.

First, there is a declaration—
a statement of release.
A line in the sand.
A search for peace.

Forgetting pain is impossible.
Reminders come tenfold.
Moving on in an instant,
no man has done it before.

Love is a battlefield, they say.
We fight gladly, with our best plans made
until we're left standing, with our hearts in our hands,
wondering how we even got this way.

Familiarities

There was a time we had it right.
There was a time when everything seemed perfect.
There was a time you held me tight.

I don't even miss you,
I don't even want you.
I just miss how you knew me, and I you.

Every freckle,
every wrinkle,
every mood I learned to handle.

Both of us predictable.
Both of us lost.
Both of us hurting.
Both of us missing everything that once was.

4am

It's 4am.
The sting of loneliness is bitter and cold.
I lay sideways, trying to fill the space that once held you.
I waste no time wishing you were here,
If only for comfort and freedom from pain and fear.

4:11
It's easy to wonder if leaving was the right thing to do.
To wonder if loneliness is something I can get through.

4:29
I realize living with silence isn't easy.
It's been years of feeling lonely,
But at least you were beside me.

4:45
I recall all we lost.
Promises were made,
vows wcrc broken.
We lied when we said, *For better or worse.*

4:59 am
I wonder if maybe I should've stayed,
living the lie that held us together,
pretending all was well,
because on dark, lonely nights, I still wish you were still here.

All this time

All this time
I knew it wasn't right—
But oh, I wanted to try.

Maybe I was young
at both heart and mind—
I didn't communicate right.

We were both broken,
both of us stubborn—
Too much alike.

Drifting apart came easy.
You decided not to want me.
I decided not to stay.

Neither of us perfect.
Neither of us whole.
.Neither healed enough to love each other right.

Time finally found us.
What we built couldn't hold,
although we thought we'd get by.

Time doesn't heal all—
sometimes it wrecks us
with no end to loneliness in sight.

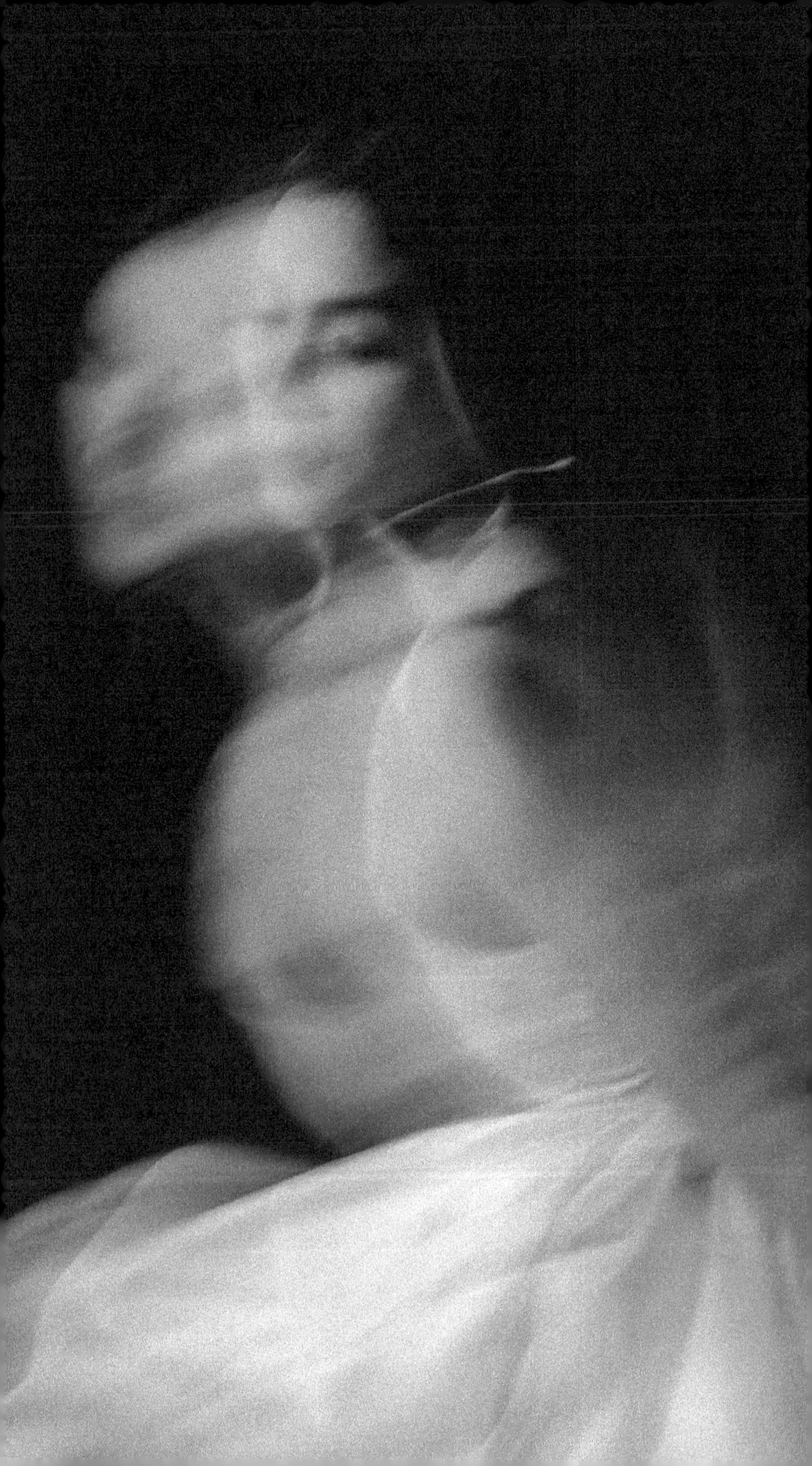

Haunted

I've been happy and living with no regrets.
My life's been good, my heart full.
The Lord knows I've been blessed.

But I'm haunted.
In the middle of the night, or when stopped at a red light,
your memory seeps through.

Most of the time, feeling content is enough.
Most of the time, moving forward is done with grace.
But all my memories contain your face.

But it's not your face that haunts me—
it's the words once spoken between us.
All the love we made.

And the love, we cannot recreate.

When

When I see families together on the holidays,
doing holiday things, I am sick with envy.

When I see anniversaries,
I wonder if they had the same problems as us.

When I see the ones who have found what's right,
I am angry that I haven't.

When I see the ones who are sure,
I wonder how they ever got there.

When our children's eyes light up
when you walk in the room, I feel doubt.

When tears of heartache roll down my face,
I cry some more as I wipe them away.

When does the doubt begin to fade and the healing begin?

The End

In the end, it was all too painful.
In the end, the only option was goodbye.
The price of forgetting was just too high.
Perfection is unattainable.
We couldn't make it happen,
even with try after try.
We couldn't make the pieces fit.
Sometimes I wish I could keep you.
But in the end, it's still *goodbye*.

Realization

For a moment, I tried believing this all was a mistake.
As if things just all of a sudden went south.
Can we turn back around?

Was the situation misjudged?
Was my mind skewing the memories of us?

Then I remembered that love had soured long ago.
And I was tired.
And my heart really was broken.

No, I left you on purpose.
This is now a battleground.

IV.

DEPRESSION

Useful tips for getting through a divorce:

- Eat something healthy and good for you.
- The next few days, eat like shit. Better yet, hardly eat at all.
- Get up early and start your day with a positive mindset.
- Lay in bed, tossing and turning for a full 24-hour period
- Only get up to care for the children.
- Go to the gym.
- Go to the store and impulse buy everything you don't need.
- Start your day by getting dressed up—try to feel pretty again.
- Live in his boxers and t-shirts for a week.
- Get out and socialize—meet new people!
- Ignore all calls and texts, avoiding any plans requiring you
  to leave your house.
- Cook yourself a healthy meal.
- Use drive-throughs and contactless delivery.
- Control your emotions—keep a cool and even temper.
- Go outside to the grill in the middle of the night
  and set your wedding photos on fire.
- Write about it. Write it all down.
- Cry until your eyes are too swollen to open the next morning.
- Practice forgiveness—if only for your own sake.
- Send text messages written during moments of rage.
- Hold it all in
- Talk to a therapist
- Have faith that all things will work out.
- Have panic attacks.
- Breathe
- Scream until you are breathless

Stick with the plan. Fall apart. Live within the depths of your emotions. Rise again, feel strong, feel thankful, and wake up one morning broken again. Know that healing doesn't happen in a straight line. Die and live simultaneously each day until life decides to begin again.

Rinse and repeat.

Lost

I am lost.
Lost
at the end of the road which requires me to take a turn.

Each direction I see
is filled with bramble and covered in leaves.
The road has wavered and changed.
My heart, ripped out along the way.
Which change in direction led me astray?
I tried my best to follow the map,
and was diligent and stayed.
But now the road has brought me here.
I am so confused. I am so afraid.
I don't know who I am.

Surely this was the way?

I planned this—we had a plan.
I chose this.
We Chose this.
We paved this road.
But somehow, now I don't know the way.

Was it me or the road that changed?

Time and Again

Remodeled.
Demolished.
Never the same again.

Discarded.
Shelved.
Second best again.

Crushed.
Broken.
Disappointed again.

Uprooted.
Displaced.
Roots disturbed again.

Untethered.
Misguided.
Alone once again.

In Vain

I've been living in this nightgown for days.
It's sticky with ice cream and covered in *Lays*.
There are moments when I think I should change.
But why bother? He never noticed me anyway.

Why do anything good?
Why be faithful each day?
What's the point of striving for perfection?
It surely doesn't pay.

You can be a good wife,
living a good, Christian life,
taking care and eating right.
It all can still be taken away.

It doesn't take much—
just the promise of another's touch,
and all of a sudden,
you find that you are betrayed.

All is well though.
No need to keep your ringer on low.
The two of you can be together.
At least I am out of your way.

Moving On

Step by step, I move further away from the life we built. The one that's now in ashes. New boundaries are set. We must un-learn how married people interact.

Each new step feels awkward. Bill by bill, I remove your name as we split it all down the middle. Our lives slowly begin to unwind. Tethered for years, everything we accomplished is now in rewind.

Day by day, I miss you a little less. I don't think about the way you smell. I do not crave your touch. But some days, I wish I could crawl into your arms, if only for your familiar embrace.

Box by box, our home begins to empty. The plates, the books, the toys, and the pictures. Everything will get shipped away and put back in place within different walls, on a different street, in different ways.

To a new home where I don't want to be.

Each decision I make alone feels more unsure. I no longer require your opinion— it's your assuredness that I need.

Every minute, every feeling, every milestone— it all seems empty without you here. I get by, but with no real sense of direction. I am moving on, but at the same time, standing still.

Ending a painful era is still an ending, so it all hurts the same.

Single Mom

While hiding my bare, left ring finger
underneath my crossed arms,
I can almost hear the gossip
rolling off their tongues.

As I walk through this party for kids,
they're all wondering where my husband is
and why there's a for sale sign on the lawn,
taking note of how often I've been alone.

All the dads chat in a circle.
Now that crowd is thinner.
I'm the only one holding piñata bags
and taking all the pictures

With pity in their eyes,
folks ask how we're doing.
Doing okay, I lie,
hidden tears accruing.

Dying Inside

Today, all I can do is cry
while lying in bed.
Our entire relationship was a lie.

I sob as it all comes to mind.
Curled up in a ball,
I know we're losing it all.

The curtains consume the light
as I move like a slug
through the room where we once made love.

A Lonely World

Our world is lonely,
and I must carry this all on my own.
And it's daunting to know
that it all lands on me.

Whether everyone succeeds,
whether everyone is happy,
Whether I meet all their needs.

As you pull away even more,
clarity grows
as I begin to realize
We are a family no more.

Nothingness

I am sitting in the middle of the unknown,
staring down at what looks like nothingness.
Everything we built is gone.
The awareness of what was to come,
is what kept me playing it safe all along.

And now I am here.
Motionless, waiting for a sign.
I was sad while I was in it,
and sad on the other side.

I see the nothingness before me,
but all I can do is stare.
Hands out,
feet planted in the ground,
and not an answer in sight.

Falling Apart

The worst thing
about falling apart,
is that for everyone else,
life goes on.

Bills still come in.
Dishes need to be washed.
There is no respite
for the weathered and worn.

Friends send up prayers—
Well wishes and condolences,
carrying on with their own lives,
all while inside, you're dying.

V.
ACCEPTANCE

Death By Growth

Welcome to my funeral—
Open casket. Wide-open

so you can see the damage,
the wreckage,
and the makeup, covering it all up.

Do not cry,
for I am in a better place.

This woman lies lifeless—
the one you once knew.

And although now, she feels cold,
she's not actually dead,

but in a self-curated cocoon,
awaiting her transformation,
building everything anew.

When she awakes,
and the transformation has taken place,
you will no longer know her.

Her words, her actions, her standards—
nothing will be the same.

Self-reflection killed her,
but the darkness will bring her back to life.

Quitter

Call me a quitter and I won't deny it.
I quit a lot of things.
I quit allowing myself to be lied to,
and I quit allowing myself to accept less than what I was giving.
I quit allowing myself to go on pretending
everything was well.

Call me selfish and I won't prove you wrong.
I quit stalling and hesitating.
I quit loving someone else more than I loved myself,
and I quit taking each day for granted.
I quit allowing myself to say no to the things I wanted.

Instead, I started looking out for myself.

Breaking Away

Each day, I began to flip my phone over less.
I stopped unlocking it to be sure I hadn't missed a message.

The arguing ceased.
Sleep came easier.

No more sleepless nights, wondering where you are,
or who she is, or why she is in your arms.

I stopped looking for your car in all your normal places.
The cracks in my heart began to fill.

Words exchanged between us have lost their sting.
My faith grows stronger. I fret over nothing.

Sometimes, the pain underneath still bubbles to the surface.
There were times when I didn't know if I would make it.

Today I am here.
Still unhealed.

Complete nonetheless,
as the lessons begin to take form.

Jump

You ask me, How

How what? I say.

How did you find the courage to leave?

I can only put it like this:
I closed my eyes, squeezed my nose, and I jumped.

No longer worrying about whether the water is deep enough,
no longer afraid of what lies beneath,
I just took the leap.

Once I landed, I took one small step at a time.
Eventually, my steps grew bolder,
and longer in stride.

The farther away I walked, the more it felt right.
Before too long, I looked back and I wondered;

How did I ever stay for so many nights?

I Finally Stopped

I finally stopped
chasing,
fighting,
crying,
and being too much for you.

I decided to
listen to myself,
call out the lies,
Started looking within,
and started to break away.

Then you started
packing,
cussing,
fighting,
and losing your mind.

Now I will
call back my power,
have faith in myself,
break the cycle,

and begin to love again.

Cutting The Cord

Years of concentration
securing life's cord to you,
Attempting to strengthen the bonds over time

I was killing myself, trying to love you,
until I asked myself,
What value can I offer if I'm dying?

I began to clearly see
how detached I had been from myself—
how broken I had become.

I was holding onto this life so tightly,
then I looked down and saw the damage,
and realized it was time to let go.

I saw that the cord was decaying
so I panicked and cut the cord with a dull knife,
and I was pulled away in an instant,
and I floundered and floated away.

No longer having a cord to hold onto,
I felt like I was drowning.
I couldn't find my footing or catch my breath.

But before too long,
I began to feel my own heart beating,
and realized I was thriving.

For the first time, I felt like myself.
Like I could trust myself.
Like I deserved to love myself.

I felt alive for the first time since
I cannot even remember.
I started to see how this was all a blessing,

and how I had grown,
and found wisdom,
and found my own way.

This breaking within me saved me.
This is a new beginning.
This is a renewed life.

A Dream For a Dream

The water only rises for a season.
The pain eventually must stop.
You're just trading a dream for a dream—
the outcome is a brand new person.

For where would we be without our stories
of how we overcame?
Of how we found redemption
after getting through all the rain?

A whirlwind doesn't blow without a reason
The ground is not prone to shake
when all things fall to pieces—
it is quite literally for Heaven's sake.

Within the moments

Balance is a treasure we all seek.
In the end, we are fruitless.

But in the act of seeking,
we find answers to life's other truths.

Like what we are made of,
and what we can get through.

Truth says we are strong enough.
The biggest truth is we are magic.

Through love, we learn what to give.
Pain teaches us what to hold back.

And if we are wise,
every moment becomes something beautiful.

Changes

I'll never be the same again.
My youth has gone away.

I'll never be the same again.
I'm jaded and betrayed.

I'll never be the same again,
I have children I must raise.

I'll never be the same again,
My life is in disarray. . .

I'll never be the same again.
I won my life back.

I'll never be the same again.
My freedom is now intact.

I'll never be the same again.
I admire all my cracks.

I'll never be the same again.
Damaged, but never broken.

With me, my heart is safe.

New Beginnings

No wisdom can be obtained from the storm
we did not go through.
So, therefore, we must be just as grateful
for the rain as we are for the sunshine.
We need them both for all of life's various seasons.

With pain comes change.
With change comes experience.
With experience comes wisdom.
With wisdom comes new sight
With new sight comes growth.
With growth comes fresh ideas.
With fresh ideas comes improvement.
With improvement comes peace.

And finally, we walk through life knowing more,
able to feel more deeply,
and with all the new beginnings we are blessed with.

Resolution

It's times like these, when life is tossing you about,
that you uncover new sources of resilience
that had been hidden within you.

It's times like these when you learn what's fake and
what's real. And who, for that matter.

It's not a test, but reassurance from God and the
Universe, that not only do they have your back,
but they get to show off a little too.

It's the everyday miracles— the unexpected peace
as you go through the storm, and the love you
receive from the real ones that keep us all going.

Somehow, we will all get through this crazy,
wild thing called life.

DEARLY DIVORCED,

We are gathered here today to find clarity, heal, grow, and accept the decisions we have made. Our hearts may be broken, but through the brokenness, we hope to find peace. We will create new paths for our life as we ride the waves, dodge the curveballs, and sit through our pain.

Tomorrow is a mystery, but also a gift. What we have is a blank slate before us—room to grow. We must have faith that what grows from pain is often extraordinarily beautiful. There has been, and will still be, a lot of emotion that will need to be sifted through. We must channel this energy as we move through our sadness.

Allow yourself to grieve dear friend. Grieve for all that you have lost. But don't stay there. Shed your tears. Set the flowers down at the grave of that which once was, visit on occasion if you must, but don't you dare linger. Along with the flowers, you must set down all the guilt and should-haves and the things gone wrong. Get up and leave that grave behind. Don't give what is dead any power.

We will learn. We will grow. We will love again.

Starting today, with ourselves.